-aw as in paw

Pam Scheunemann

Consulting Editor Monica Marx, M.A./Reading Specialist

Published by SandCastle™, an imprint of ABDO Publishing Company, 4940 Viking Drive, Edina, Minnesota 55435.

Printed in the United States.

Credits
Edited by: Pam Price
Curriculum Coordinator: Nancy Tuminelly
Cover and Interior Design and Production: Mighty Media
Photo Credits: Brand X Pictures, Comstock, Corbis Images, Digital Vision, Hemera, Image 100, PhotoDisc, Stockbyte

Library of Congress Cataloging-in-Publication Data

Scheunemann, Pam, 1955-
    -Aw as in paw / Pam Scheunemann.
        p. cm. -- (Word families. Set VII)
    Summary: Introduces, in brief text and illustrations, the use of the letter combination "aw" in such words as "paw," "saw," "gnaw," and "flaw."
    ISBN 1-59197-263-9
    1. Readers (Primary) [1. Vocabulary. 2. Reading.] I. Title. II. Series.

PE1119 .S4345 2003
428.1--dc21   2002038216

SandCastle™ books are created by a professional team of educators, reading specialists, and content developers around five essential components that include phonemic awareness, phonics, vocabulary, text comprehension, and fluency. All books are written, reviewed, and leveled for guided reading, early intervention reading, and Accelerated Reader® programs and designed for use in shared, guided, and independent reading and writing activities to support a balanced approach to literacy instruction.

Let Us Know

After reading the book, SandCastle would like you to tell us your stories about reading. What is your favorite page? Was there something hard that you needed help with? Share the ups and downs of learning to read. We want to hear from you! To get posted on the ABDO Publishing Company Web site, send us e-mail at:

sandcastle@abdopub.com

SandCastle Level: Transitional

-aw Words

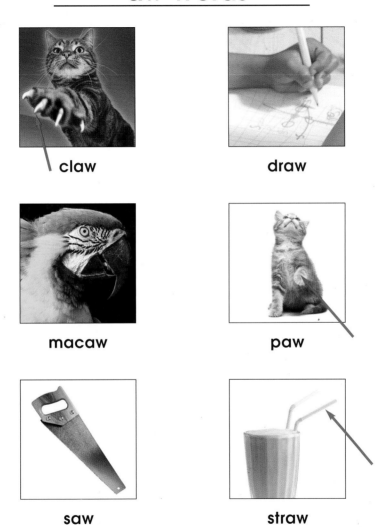

claw

draw

macaw

paw

saw

straw

3

Koko uses each claw
to hold on.

Rod and Mike like to
draw.

Pepper is a macaw.

The kitten put its paw
on the cat.

Ben and Lola learn
how to use the saw.

Elle wears a straw hat.

The Magic Claw

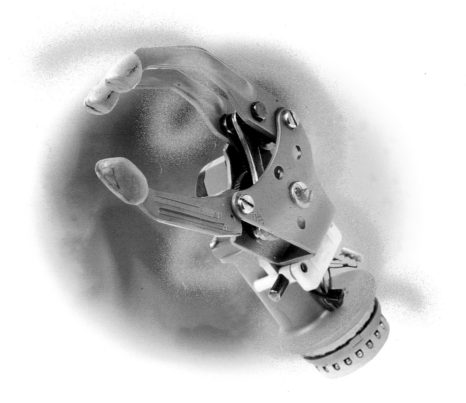

Tom invented
a magic claw.

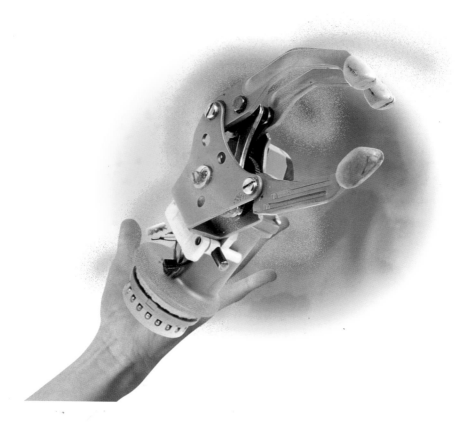

He learned to use it
without a flaw.

scratch
scratch

The magic claw can
scratch his jaw.

The magic claw
can use a saw.

The magic claw
can also draw.

It picks a crab up
by its claw.

It even holds
Tom's macaw.

The magic claw
wears a hat of straw.

The magic claw
holds a kitten's paw.

Tom always knew
it was a magic claw.

He is still surprised
by what he saw!

The -aw Word Family

caw	macaw
claw	paw
draw	raw
flaw	saw
gnaw	seesaw
jaw	slaw
jigsaw	straw
law	thaw

Glossary

Some of the words in this list may have more than one meaning. The meaning listed here reflects the way the word is used in the book.

claw   a sharp, curved nail on the foot of an animal; the pincer at the end of a lobster or crab's leg

flaw   a fault or imperfection

macaw   a long-tailed, brightly colored parrot of Central or South America

paw   the foot of a four-legged animal that has claws

straw   a slender tube you can drink through

About SandCastle™

A professional team of educators, reading specialists, and content developers created the SandCastle™ series to support young readers as they develop reading skills and strategies and increase their general knowledge. The SandCastle™ series has four levels that correspond to early literacy development in young children. The levels are provided to help teachers and parents select the appropriate books for young readers.

Emerging Readers
(no flags)

Beginning Readers
(1 flag)

Transitional Readers
(2 flags)

Fluent Readers
(3 flags)

These levels are meant only as a guide. All levels are subject to change.

To see a complete list of SandCastle™ books and other nonfiction titles from ABDO Publishing Company, visit www.abdopub.com or contact us at:

4940 Viking Drive, Edina, Minnesota 55435 • 1-800-800-1312 • fax: 1-952-831-1632